Happy Birthday Grandmother

奶奶，
生日快樂！

Kathleen R. Seaton 著

姚 紅 繪

"Today is Grandmother's birthday,"
Grandfather said.

"Let's have a party!" Little Brother said.

"I will *bake a cake," Mother said.

"I will buy her a present," Father said.

*為生字，請參照生字表

"I will buy her a *lovely hat," Big Sister said.

"I will buy her a book," Big Brother said.

"I will buy her..." I began.

"Don't worry," said Little Sister.

"Big Sister will help you."

"She is the shopping queen,"

Grandfather said, with a smile.

6

Off we went.

Big Sister showed me many beautiful things.

Still I could not decide and soon it was time to go home.

TOY SHOP

CHOCOLATE

9

"But I don't have a present for grandmother, " I cried.
"Sorry," said Big Brother.
"But we can't be late for Grandmother's party."

10

Then, I saw the most beautiful flowers in the world.

"There!" I *shouted. "There's the *perfect present."

Happily, I went home with Grandmother's present.

"Where's Grandmother?" I cried.

"I'm sorry," Mother said. "Grandmother *has a bad cold. She must stay *upstairs today."

"Oh no!" everyone cried.

"We can have a party another day," Grandfather said.

"We can save our presents for another day," Big Sister said.

"Can the cake wait too?" Little Brother asked.

"Yes !" everyone laughed.

"Everything can wait until Grandmother is *better."

"But my present!" I cried. "My present can't wait!

Can I take them to her?"

"I'm sorry," Father said.

"You might *catch a cold, too."

*Suddenly, I had an idea.

"Big Brother, can you shout a *message

to Grandmother?"

"*Of course," Big Brother *replied. "What is it?"

"Ask her to go to her window at three o'clock," I said.

17

I ran as fast as I could and bought two big balloons.

Then, I tied the flowers to them and stood below

Grandmother's window.

At three o'clock, Grandmother *waved from

her window.

18

"Happy Birthday, Grandmother!" I *called.

I let go of the balloons.

Up, up, up they went carrying

the most beautiful flowers to

the *best Grandmother in the world.

生字表

adj.=形容詞，adv.=副詞，n.=名詞，v.=動詞

奶奶，生日快樂！

p.2-3
爺爺說：「今天是奶奶的生日。」
弟弟說：「我們來辦個慶生會吧！」

p.4-5
媽媽說：「我會烤個蛋糕。」
爸爸說：「我會買個禮物給她。」
姊姊說：「我會買頂漂亮的帽子給她。」
哥哥說：「我會買本書給她。」

p.6-7
我開口說：「我會買……」
妹妹說：「別擔心，姊姊會幫你挑的。」
爺爺帶著笑容說：「她可是購物女王喔！」

p.8-9
於是我們出發了。
姊姊給我看了好多漂亮的東西，但是，我還是無法決定要選哪一個作禮物。很快的，回家的時間到了。

p.10-11

我大叫：「但是我沒買到奶奶的生日禮物！」

哥哥說：「抱歉，但奶奶的慶生會我們不能遲到啊！」

這時候，我看到了全世界最美麗的花。我大叫：「就是那個！那就是最完美的禮物！」

我快樂的帶著奶奶的生日禮物回家了。

p.12-13

我大叫：「奶奶呢？」

媽媽說：「真抱歉，奶奶得了重感冒。她今天必須待在樓上。」

大家大叫：「喔，不！」

p.14-15

爺爺說：「我們可以改天再辦慶生會。」

姊姊說：「我們可以留著禮物，改天再送。」

弟弟說：「那蛋糕也可以等嗎？」

大家笑著說：「可以呀！一切都可以等到奶奶康復再說。」

p.16-17

我大叫:「可是我的禮物不能等！我可以拿給她嗎？」

爸爸說:「抱歉！你可能也會感冒的。」

我突然想到一個點子。「哥哥，你可不可以大聲的告訴奶奶一件事？」

哥哥回答:「當然可以，是什麼事呢？」

我說:「請她三點的時候走到她的窗邊。」

p.18-19

我以最快的速度跑出去買了兩個氣球。

然後，我把花綁在氣球上，站在奶奶的窗戶下等。

三點的時候，奶奶從她的窗戶向我揮揮手。

p.20-21

我大喊:「奶奶，生日快樂！」我放開了氣球。

它們就一直往上飄啊飄的，帶著世界上最漂亮的花，送給世界上最棒的奶奶。

英文練習

小班的奶奶生日到了！不過，大家各準備了什麼禮物送給奶奶呢？跟著下面的提示作答，你就會知道答案囉！

❶ 奶奶收到的禮物

請聽 CD Track 4，跟著唸出下面的單字：

a book

a cake

a hat

some flowers

❷ 請聽朗讀CD的 Track 5，並將答案填入以下的空格內

1. I will buy her
   _____.

2. I will bake her
   _____.

3. I will buy her
   _____.

4. I will buy her
   _____.

　　答案都寫好了嗎？接下來，請再聽一次CD的Track 5，複習一下剛剛練習的句子。要跟著CD一起大聲的唸出來喔！

　　　　　　　　　　　　　　正確答案在第 29 頁喔！

27

你的生日是幾號？

小朋友，你記得所有家人的生日嗎？如果不知道的話，趕快去調查一下，然後把大家的生日和年齡填入下面這張表吧！在家人生日的那天，記得要跟他們說聲 Happy Birthday 唷！

● 爺爺的名字是＿＿＿＿＿＿，生日是民國＿＿＿＿年＿＿月＿＿日，今年＿＿＿＿歲。

● 奶奶的名字是＿＿＿＿＿＿，生日是民國＿＿＿＿年＿＿月＿＿日，今年＿＿＿＿歲。

● 外公的名字是＿＿＿＿＿＿，生日是民國＿＿＿＿年＿＿月＿＿日，今年＿＿＿＿歲。

● 外婆的名字是＿＿＿＿＿＿，生日是民國＿＿＿＿年＿＿月＿＿日，今年＿＿＿＿歲。

● 爸爸的名字是＿＿＿＿＿＿，生日是民國＿＿＿＿年＿＿月＿＿日，今年＿＿＿＿歲。

● 媽媽的名字是＿＿＿＿＿＿，生日是民國＿＿＿＿年＿＿月＿＿日，今年＿＿＿＿歲。

● 我在家裡 □ 是爸爸媽媽唯一的寶貝。
　　　　　 □ 排行第＿＿＿＿，我有＿＿＿＿個哥哥，＿＿＿＿個姊姊，＿＿＿＿個弟弟，＿＿＿＿個妹妹。

接下來，請將你的兄弟姊妹的生日一一起完成！

_____的
名字是_____
生日是民國
____年____月____日
今年____歲。

_____的
名字是_____
生日是民國
____年____月____日
今年____歲。

_____的
名字是_____
生日是民國
____年____月____日
今年____歲。

_____的
名字是_____
生日是民國
____年____月____日
今年____歲。

我的名字是_____
生日是民國
_____年_____月_____日
今年_____歲。

29

Kathleen R. Seaton is an Associate Professor in the Department of Foreign Languages and Literature at Tunghai University. She teaches a seminar course in Children's Literature, Film and Culture, courses in composition and oral practice and electives in acting and drama. She holds an interdisciplinary PhD in Mass Communication and an MFA in Film from Ohio University, Athens Ohio, U.S.A.

Kathleen R. Seaton （呂珍妮） 在東海大學外國語文學系擔任副教授。她教授兒童文學、電影與文化的文學討論課程，另外還開設英文作文和口語訓練兩堂主修課程，選修課程方面則有表演與戲劇。她擁有美國俄亥俄大學的大眾傳播學跨領域博士和電影藝術碩士學位。

寫書的人

　　姚紅畢業於南京藝術學院中國畫系，現職於江蘇少年兒童出版社，從事兒童繪本的編輯和創作多年。她的繪畫作品《蓬蓬頭溜冰的故事》獲第四屆中國優秀少年讀物一等獎；《牙印兒》獲國際兒童讀物聯盟「小松樹」獎；《飛吻大王》獲第五屆國家圖書獎。由姚紅策劃並與他人合作編輯的《「我真棒」幼兒成長圖畫書》獲 2000 年冰心兒童圖書獎。

畫畫的人

I Love My Family Series

我愛我的家 系列

Kathleen R. Seaton 著／姚紅 繪

附中英雙語朗讀 CD
適讀對象：學習英文 0～2 年者（國小 1～3 年級適讀）

六本全新創作的中英雙語繪本，
六個溫馨幽默的故事，
帶領小朋友們進入單純可愛的小班的生活，
跟他一起分享和家人之間親密的感情！

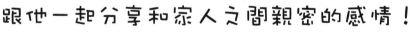

國家圖書館出版品預行編目資料

Happy Birthday Grandmother:奶奶, 生日快樂! /
Kathleen R. Seaton著;姚紅繪;本局編輯部譯.－
－初版一刷.－－臺北市：三民，2006
　　面；　　公分.－－(Fun心讀雙語叢書.我愛我的
家系列)
中英對照
ISBN 957－14－4423－5　　(精裝)

1.英國語言－讀本

523.38　　　　　　　　　　　　　　94026446

網路書店位址　http://www.sanmin.com.tw

© **Happy Birthday Grandmother**
—— 奶奶, 生日快樂!

著作人　Kathleen R. Seaton
繪　者　姚　紅
譯　者　本局編輯部
發行人　劉振強
著作財
產權人　三民書局股份有限公司
　　　　臺北市復興北路386號
發行所　三民書局股份有限公司
　　　　地址／臺北市復興北路386號
　　　　電話／(02)25006600
　　　　郵撥／0009998－5
印刷所　三民書局股份有限公司
門市部　復北店／臺北市復興北路386號
　　　　重南店／臺北市重慶南路一段61號
初版一刷　2006年1月
編　號　S 806061
定　價　新臺幣壹佰捌拾元整
行政院新聞局登記證局版臺業字第○二○○號

ISBN　957-14-4423-5　　(精裝)